Beagle

Charles and Linda George

Created by Q2AMedia
www.q2amedia.com
Editor Jeff O' Hare
Publishing Director Chester Fisher
Client Service Manager Santosh Vasudevan
Project Manager Kunal Mehrotra
Art Director Harleen Mehta
Designer Divij Singh
Picture Researcher Nivisha Sinha

Library of Congress Cataloging-in-Publication Data
Beagle / [Charles George,Linda George].
p. cm. — (Top dogs)
Includes index.
ISBN 0-531-23242-5/ 978-0-531-23242-2 (hardcover)
1. Beagle (Dog breed)—Juvenile literature. I. Title. II. Series.
SF429.B3B433 2010
636.753'7—dc22
2010035020

Printed and bound in Heshan, China
232580 10/10
10 9 8 7 6 5 4 3 2 1

Picture Credits
t= top, b= bottom, c= center, r= right, l= left

Cover Page: Carl Fleming/Istockphoto.

Title Page: Rafael Angel Garcia Dobarganes/Shutterstock.

4-5: Miroslav K/Shutterstock; 5: Micka/Dreamstime; 6-7: Pascal Pamme/Fotolia; 7: Kodo/Dreamstime; 8: Dra Schwartz/Istockphoto; 9: Verityjohnson/Shutterstock; 10-11: Carrie Bottomley/Istockphoto; 12: Purestock/Photolibrary; 13: Purestock/Photolibrary; 14: Monika Wisniewska/Shutterstock; 15: Vesna Cvorovic/Shutterstock, Simone Van Den Berg/Shutterstock; 16: Rhonda O Donnell/Shutterstock; 17: Rafael Angel Garcia Dobarganes/Shutterstock; 18: Arenacreative/Dreamstime; 19: Sadeugra/Istockphoto; 20-21: Masterfile Corporation; 22-23: Christopher Jacobson/Bigstock; 23: Dean Bertoncelj/Dreamstime; 24: Brad Sauter/Dreamstime, Paul Matthew Photography/Shutterstock; 25: Juniors Bildarchiv/Photolibrary; 26-27: Arena Creative/Shutterstock; 28: David Hartley/Rex Features; 29: Gary Martin/Istockphoto; 30: China Foto Press/Getty Images; 31: Buena Vista/Everett/Rex Features.

Contents

What are Beagles?

Beagles (*bee-gulls*) are small, happy dogs. They make wonderful pets. They have a great sense of smell. A beagle can use its sense of smell to track and find animals. Sometimes they are even used to find people!

Fast Fact

Beagles belong to a group of dogs called Scenthounds.

Beagles came to the U.S. from England in the mid-1800s. They have short legs. Their small size lets them find and dig out small animals such as rabbits.

Fast Fact

The name "beagle" comes from an old word that means "small."

Shetlands

Orkneys

Hebrides

Scotland

England

Northern Ireland

North East

North West

Isle of Man

Yorkshire & the Humber

Ireland

Anglesey

East Midlands

West Midlands

East of England

Wales

London

South West

South East

Isles of Scilly

Isle of Wight

Channel Islands

Everyone Loves Beagles!

Beagles are great family pets. They are **loyal** and loving. They like to spend some time inside and some time outside every day.

Fast Fact

All dogs require some **training**. Training helps them get along well with children.

Beagles love to **explore** outdoors, where they can pick up a **scent** and follow it. They get excited when they are **tracking** small animals. When they are excited, they bay. This is a loud dog noise. It is easy to know when beagles are baying.

Fast Fact

Because they are so friendly, beagles need less training than most other dogs.

Beagles Love Kids!

Beagles get along well with children. They are gentle with very small children. Beagles usually won't nip or bite when a child pats a little too hard or pulls their tails.

Fast Fact

Beagles are friendly. But any dog will bite if you are mean to it.

Beagles love to play outdoors. They like chasing a ball or just running. Beagles love to swim. They also like playing games like fetch and tug-of-war.

Fast Fact

Try hiding one of your beagle's favorite toys. How quickly did it sniff out where you hid the toy?

Puppy Love

Beagle puppies weigh about 7 to 10 ounces (0.2-0.3 kg) at birth. The average **litter** size is 4 to 5. A beagle mother keeps her litter warm. She lets them **nurse** for six weeks. Then, they can start eating puppy food.

Fast Fact

When a beagle puppy curls up to sleep, it's about the size of a bagel.

Beagle puppies love to play really hard, and then take a nap. Soon they are up to play again. They like to nip at other dogs' legs, necks, and ears.

Fast Fact

Beagle puppies are very small. It is easy to keep them in a safe place. When they get bigger, they can climb out of their box in a flash!

Choosing a Beagle Puppy

Do you live in a small place? A beagle puppy may be perfect for you. A beagle doesn't need a lot of room. It may be playful, but it won't get as excited as some other dog breeds.

Fast Fact

Beagles like to be with other dogs or with people.

How do you choose a puppy? Think about your family. A male beagle has lots of energy. You may want a female beagle if you have a quiet family.

Taking Care of Your Beagle Puppy

Your puppy will enjoy eating dog food that's made just for puppies. You should always have clean, cool water for your puppy to drink.

Fast Fact

Table food is not good for puppies.

Fast Fact

Puppies chew on things to make their new teeth feel better. Their mouths hurt when they are **teething**.

Your puppy's teeth will soon start growing. It needs something to chew on. Give your puppy a chew toy. It will be less likely to chew on your shoes. Never let your puppy chew on anything that might hurt it!

How Big do Beagles Get?

Adult beagles grow to be about 13 to 15 inches (33-38 cm) tall. They usually weigh between 18 and 30 pounds (8.2-13.6 kg). Females weigh less than males.

Fast Fact

Some beagles are even smaller. "Pocket" beagles can be less than 8 inches (20.3 cm) tall.

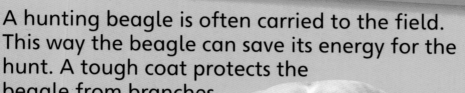

A hunting beagle is often carried to the field. This way the beagle can save its energy for the hunt. A tough coat protects the beagle from branches and rocks. Its short legs let it go under bushes with ease.

Fast Fact

A beagle is fairly small. It is easy to keep up with a beagle when it's tracking.

Brushing Hair and Clipping Nails

Beagles have short, thick hair. This protects their skin when they are tracking. Most beagles are brown, black, and white. They **shed** mostly in spring. Beagles should be brushed every week to keep their coats shiny and free of **burrs**.

Fast Fact

All dogs enjoy a good brushing. Don't brush too hard. You might hurt them.

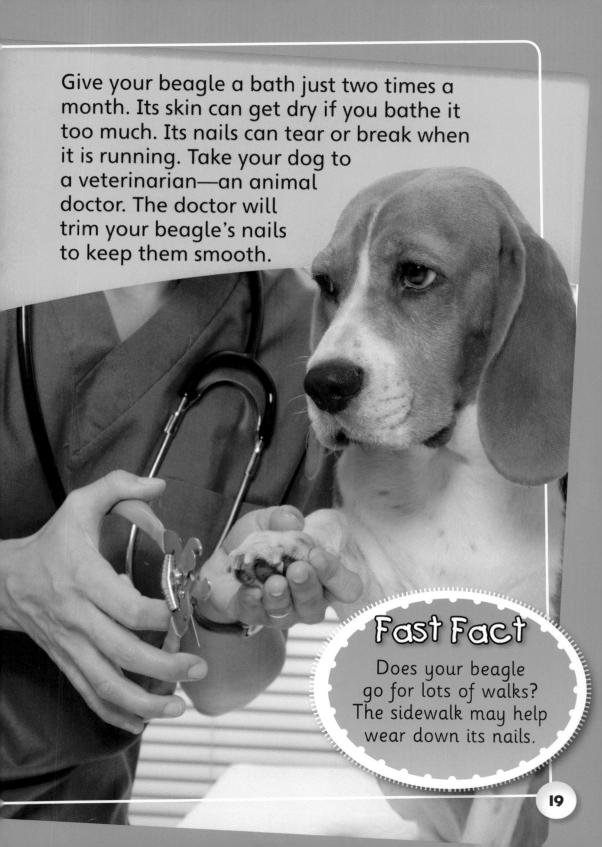

Give your beagle a bath just two times a month. Its skin can get dry if you bathe it too much. Its nails can tear or break when it is running. Take your dog to a veterinarian—an animal doctor. The doctor will trim your beagle's nails to keep them smooth.

Fast Fact

Does your beagle go for lots of walks? The sidewalk may help wear down its nails.

Sweet Beagles

Beagles make wonderful pets. They are loving and sweet. Beagles enjoy living inside the house with the people they love. A beagle puppy can become a close friend for a child.

Fast Fact

Beagles are one of the friendliest breeds of hounds.

Most beagles are quick to make friends. Even though they are friendly, they make good watchdogs. They are very smart.

Fast Fact
Beagles are always on the lookout for something new to explore.

Make Room for Your Beagle!

All beagles need room to run. It can be in a fenced backyard, on daily walks with a leash, or in a dog park. Because they like to track new scents and small animals, it's a good idea to take beagles out to the country from time to time.

Fast Fact

A beagle can hear really well. It will bay and wake you if it hears something at night.

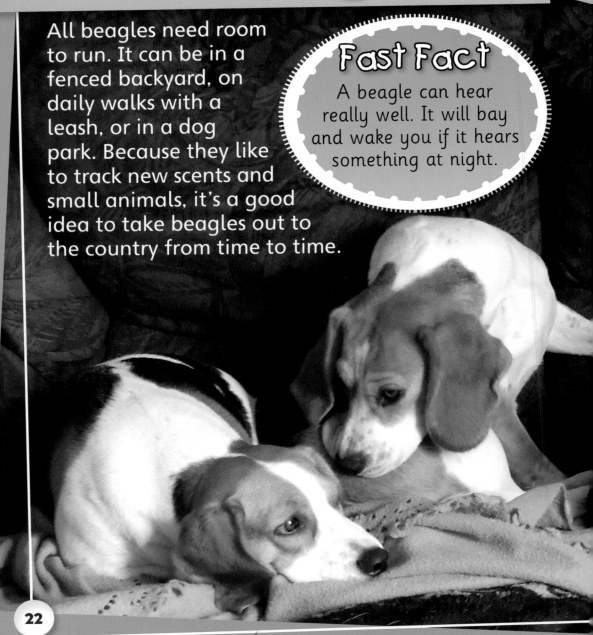

Dogs need a warm, soft place to sleep. Beagles like being close to their favorite people. Some beagles sleep at the foot of their owners' beds. Others sleep in dog beds on the floor.

Fast Fact

Does your beagle get up on the furniture? Be sure it stays on a blanket. Remember, a beagle will shed!

Loyal Friends

A beagle is like a member of your family. If someone isn't feeling well, a beagle will stay close to the sick person until they are well again. A beagle is a very loyal dog.

Fast Fact

Some beagles won't eat or drink while their owners are sick.

There is a reason beagles are loyal to their families. These dogs once ran together in groups of as many as ten while hunting. If you have only one beagle, your family becomes its group!

Fast Fact

If you've been away for a while, get ready to be licked and pawed when you get home.

Curious About Everything!

Beagles love learning new things. This makes them good trackers. They want to find the animals whose smells they sniff. They also like to taste things that look or smell good to them.

Fast Fact

A well-trained beagle can follow an animal's scent through almost anything!

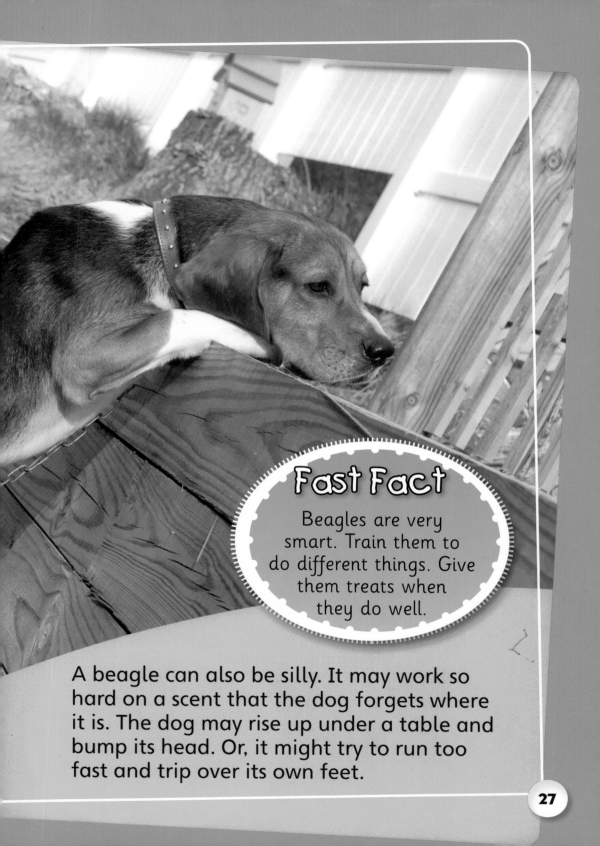

Fast Fact

Beagles are very smart. Train them to do different things. Give them treats when they do well.

A beagle can also be silly. It may work so hard on a scent that the dog forgets where it is. The dog may rise up under a table and bump its head. Or, it might try to run too fast and trip over its own feet.

Beagles Helping People

Some beagles are trained to take part in **field trials**. They compete with other beagles to see which one can best follow the trail of a rabbit. This training helps improve beagles' hunting skills.

Fast Fact

The American Kennel Club (AKC) sponsors field trials across the U.S. each year.

Because beagles are so friendly, they are often used as **therapy dogs**. These dogs visit people who live alone or who are sick. Their visits often make people feel better.

Fast Fact

Therapy dogs don't need much special training. A beagle's friendliness makes it a good therapy dog.

Best of the Breed

Fast Fact

When a beagle finds something bad in a suitcase, it will sit down. This is a signal for the suitcase to be opened and searched.

Beagles can be trained to work for the police. Beagles also work in airports. These dogs are members of the "Beagle **Brigade**." They sniff out things in people's suitcases that shouldn't be there. They find things that aren't safe.

Beagles can be seen in movies and on TV. They've also won awards. A beagle starred in the 2007 movie *Underdog*, about a beagle who had super powers. A beagle named Uno won the top award in the U.S. for **show dogs** in 2008.

Fast Fact

The most famous beagle in the world is Snoopy, the dog in the *Peanuts* cartoon strip.

Glossary

Brigade – a group that works together to do something

Burrs – seeds that stick to an animal's fur

Explore – look around a place you've never been before

Field trials – contests for dogs to see how well they can track animals

Litter – a group of puppies born to one mother, all at the same time

Loyal – faithful

Nurse – drink milk from a mother's breast

Scent – a smell

Shed – to lose hair

Teething – the growth of new teeth

Therapy – things a sick or hurt person does to get better

Track, Tracking – following a scent or other clues to try to find something

Training – lessons that are taught; teaching

Index